Zen Dogs

MEDITATIONS FOR THE WISE MINDS OF DOG LOVERS

Buddha
and the editors of
Mango Media

ISBN 978-1-63353-521-3

"My religion is very simple. My religion is Kindness."

Tenzin Gyatso, the 14th Dalai Lama

TABLE OF CONTENTS

VIRTUE   71

TRUTH   103

MIND
AND
BODY

VERSE 1

Let a wise man blow off the impurities of his self, as a smith blows off the impurities of silver one by one, little by little, and from time to time.

Becoming enlightened is not the work of a day. It is achieved in the small, steady steps we take every day.

VERSE 2

Him I call enlightened who does not offend by body, word, or thought, and is controlled on these three points.

We must strive to control the negative impulses of our bodies and minds in order to approach the world with a peaceful, loving spirit

VERSE 3

We are what we think. All that we are arises with our thoughts.

Our outlook colors our personality. Dwell on the negative, and you will appear darker. Choose optimism, and people will respond to your attitude.

VERSE 4

Fine words bear fruit in a man who acts
well in accordance with them.

Making resolutions is good, but we need to follow
our promises up with action.

VERSE 5

He who lives without looking for pleasures,
his senses well controlled, moderate in
his food, faithful and strong, him evil will
certainly not overthrow, anymore than the
wind throws down a rocky mountain.

Disciplining our bodies to resist temptation is good
practice for training our minds to resist bad influences.

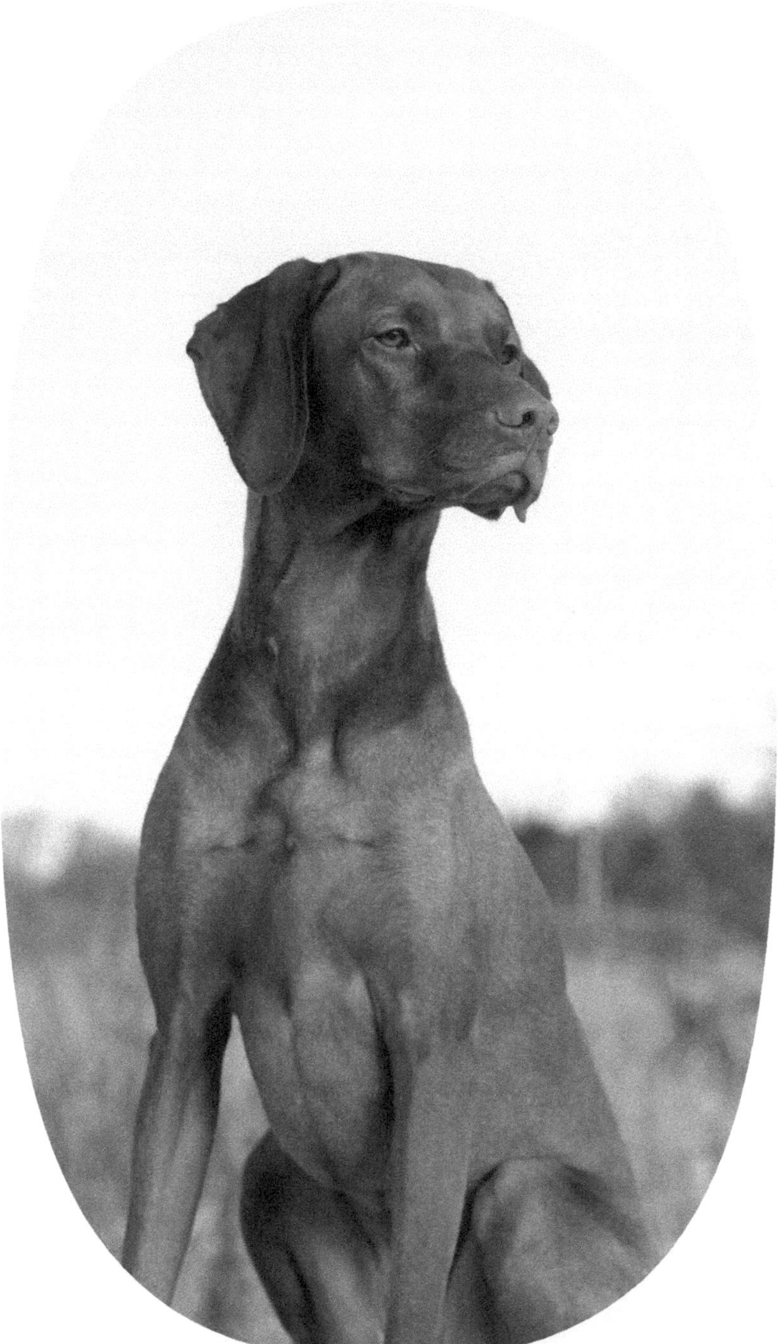

VERSE 6

Restraint in the eye is
good, good is restraint
in the ear, in the nose
restraint is good, good is
restraint in the tongue.

Our senses can bring joy, but be careful: do not to allow
them to deceive you.

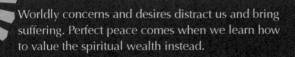

VERSE 7

The gods envy even him whose senses, like horses well broken in by the driver, have been subdued, who is free from pride and free from appetites.

Worldly concerns and desires distract us and bring suffering. Perfect peace comes when we learn how to value the spiritual wealth instead.

VERSE 8

Hunger is the worst of diseases, the body the greatest of pains; if one knows this truly, that is Nirvana, the highest happiness.

Do not allow the needs of the body to interfere with the needs of the spirit.

VERSE 9

He who overcomes this fierce thirst,
difficult to be conquered in this world,
sufferings fall off from him, like water-
drops from a lotus leaf.

We all have thirsts for more than water: for
power, for love, etc. Learning to let them go
breaks their power over us.

VERSE 10

For self is the lord of self, self is the refuge of self; therefore curb thyself as the merchant curbs a good horse.

Our bodies are temples, and so are our minds. Take care to maintain both.

VERSE 11

Careful amidst the careless,
amongst the sleeping wide-
awake, the intelligent man
leaves them all behind.

We should strive to live mindfully and spiritually, rising
above petty concerns to live more fulfilling lives.

VERSE 12

As rain breaks through an ill-thatched house, passion will break through an unreflecting mind.

We must train ourselves to resist the influence of bad habits and negative thoughts that would break us.

VERSE 13

It is good to tame the mind, which is difficult to hold in and flighty, rushing wherever it listeth; a tamed mind brings happiness.

Allowing our minds to wander causes us to miss what's happening all around us. Try to be present in each moment of your life.

VERSE 14

As the fletcher whittles and makes straight his arrows, so the master directs his straying thoughts.

Sometimes, our thoughts and emotions feel beyond our control. Remember that you have the power to change them.

VERSE 15

Therefore, the man who seeks his own welfare, should pull out this arrow—this arrow of lamentation, pain, and sorrow.

Negative emotions will not leave on their own. It is up to us to draw their poison our of our hearts.

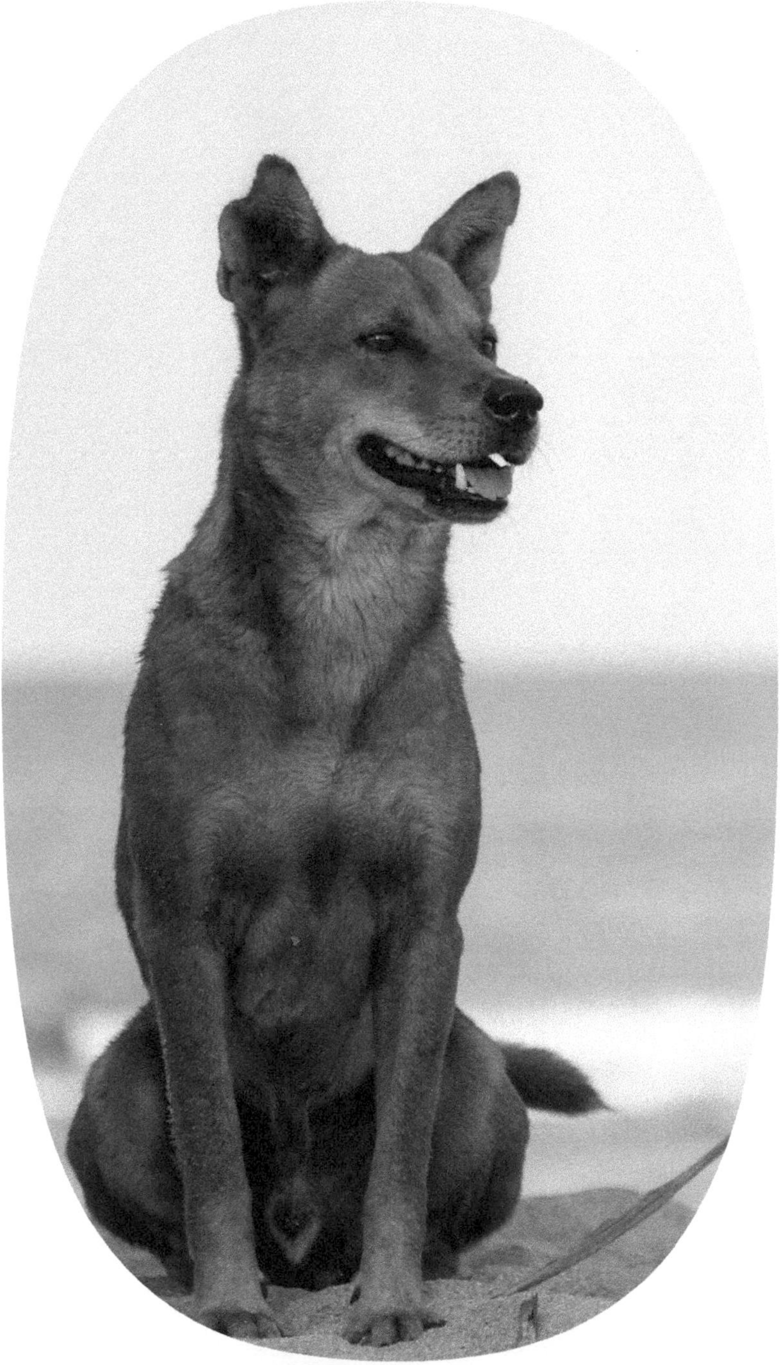

VERSE 16

A disciplined mind brings happiness.

Disciplining the mind sounds hard—even exhausting—but the peace it brings you will bring lasting happiness.

VERSE 17

However many holy words you read, However many you speak, What good will they do you If you do not act upon them?

Contemplating spiritual behaviors will not change your life. Acting on them will.

VERSE 18

Speak or act with an impure mind, And trouble will follow you.

Be careful to say what you mean. Speaking angrily in haste, or make empty promises, and you may regret it.

VERSE 19

If anything is to be done, let a man do it, let him attack it vigorously! A careless pilgrim only scatters the dust of his passions more widely.

Don't put off to tomorrow the good you could do today. There is no time like the present for good works.

VERSE 20

In making efforts to overcome wrong action, and to arouse right action, one practices Right Effort.

We can't always be perfect, but if we are constantly trying to improve with a sincere heart, then we are doing the best we can.

VERSE 21

Long is the night to him who
is awake; long is a mile to him
who is tired; long is life to the
foolish who do not know the
true law.

Life is full of ups and downs, but we will
always be supported if we live mindfully.

VERSE 22

All that we are arises with our thoughts.
With our thoughts we make the world.

Life can make you feel powerless. Learning how
to think positively and look for opportunities to
improve will help you take back your power.

VERSE 23

If one man conquer in battle a thousand times a thousand men, and if another conquers himself, he is the greatest of conquerers.

Any victory is exciting, but our greatest triumphs are the battles we win in our hearts and minds.

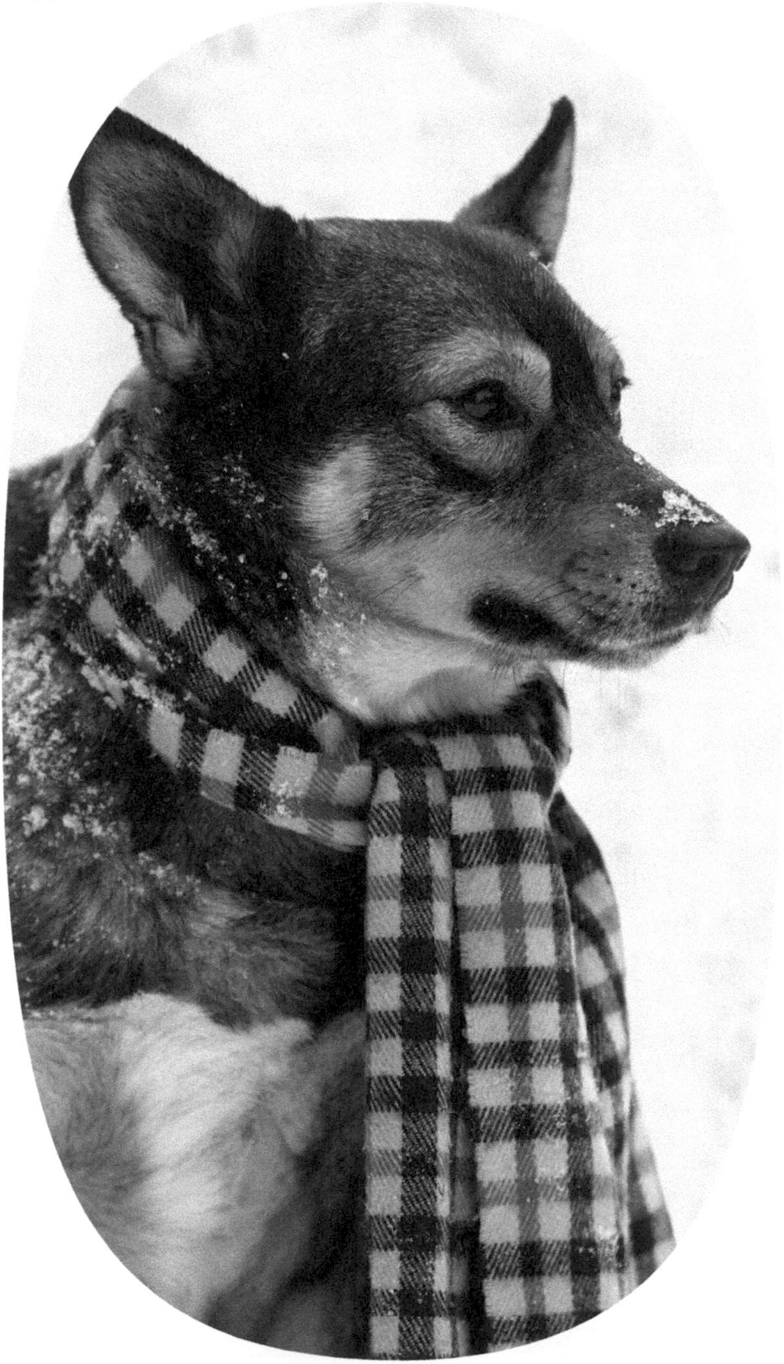

VERSE 24

How happy he is following the
path of the awakened.

Living and acting mindfully makes life a joyful journey.

HAPPINESS

VERSE 25

There is happiness in life, happiness in friendship, happiness of a family, happiness in a healthy body and mind, but when one loses them, there is suffering.

It is easy to take the small blessings of life for granted. Happiness comes from remembering to be thankful for what we have

VERSE 26

If a man speaks or acts with a pure thought, happiness follows him, like a shadow that never leaves him.

Approaching the world with optimism, kindness, and honesty brings the reward of happiness.

VERSE 27

Victory breeds hatred, for the conquered is unhappy. He who has given up both victory and defeat, he, the contented, is happy.

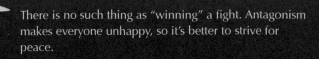

There is no such thing as "winning" a fight. Antagonism makes everyone unhappy, so it's better to strive for peace.

VERSE 28

Over Delight and Discontent one has mastery; one does not allow himself to be overcome by discontent; one subdues it, as soon as it arises.

Dwelling on the past—good or bad—holds us back. We must conquer our emotions and move forward.

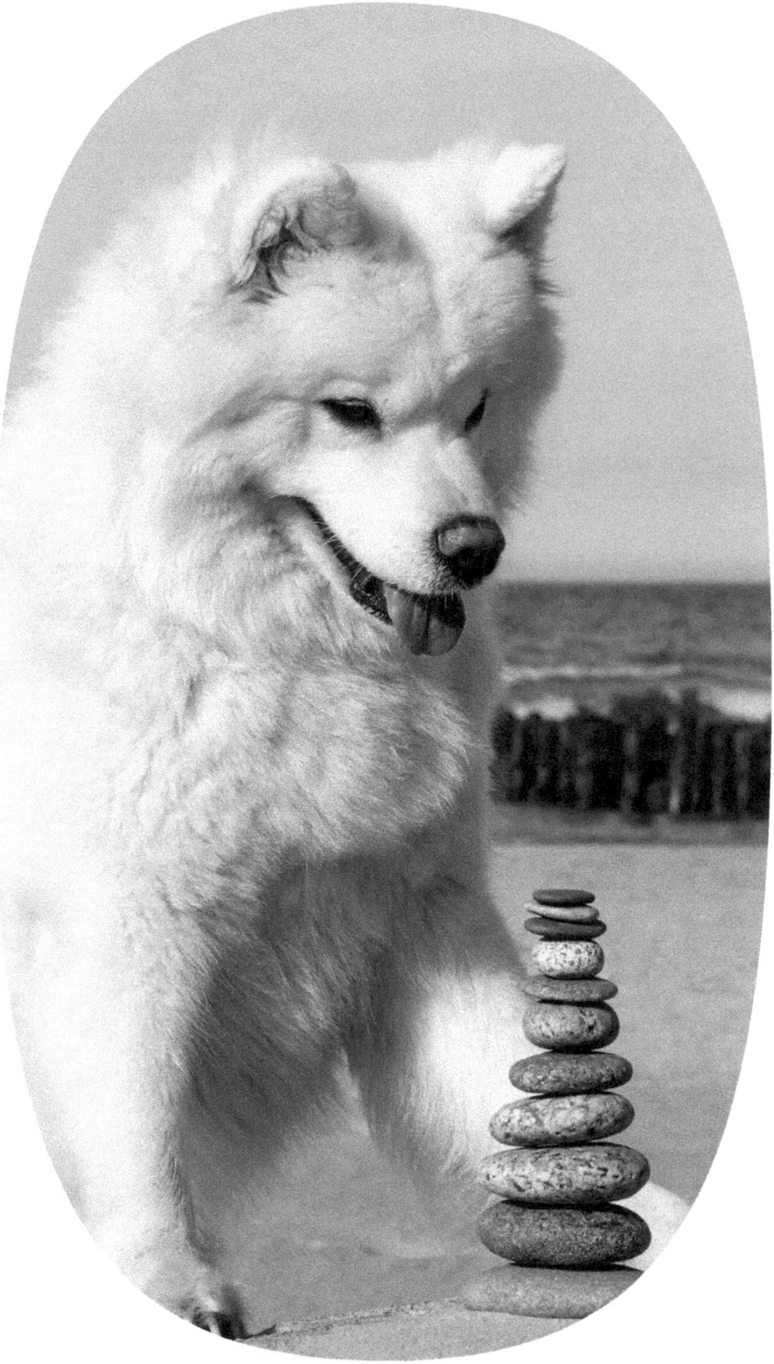

VERSE 29

Happiness or sorrow: whatever befalls you, walk on untouched, unattached.

Do not gloat in victory or sulk in defeat. Go through life with a gracious heart.

VERSE 30

He who is earnest and meditative obtains
ample joy.

Happiness comes from approaching the world
from a place of heart-felt honesty.

VERSE 31

These wise people—meditative, steady,
always possessed of strong powers
attain the highest happiness.

The best kind of happiness is the one we make by striving
to be our best selves.

VERSE 32

If by leaving a small pleasure one sees a great pleasure, let a wise man leave the small pleasure, and look to the great.

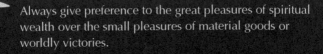

Always give preference to the great pleasures of spiritual wealth over the small pleasures of material goods or worldly victories.

VERSE 33

Let the wise man guard his thoughts,
for they are difficult to perceive, very
artful, and they rush wherever they list:
thoughts well guarded bring happiness.

Bad thoughts can come to us unbidden. It's our job
to push them away, so that they can't hurt us.

VERSE 34

Whether touched by happiness or sorrow, wise people are never depressed.

Dwelling on negativity—real or imagined—damages us. Find some joy in every day to restore happiness and tranquility.

VERSE 35

Even a good man sees evil days, as long
as his good deed has not ripened; but
when his good deed has ripened, then
does the good man see happy days.

Sometimes, it can take time to see the result of our
good works. Have patience, and know that if you do
good works that good will come back to you in time.

VERSE 36

Pleasant is virtue lasting to old age,
pleasant is a faith firmly rooted;
pleasant is attainment of intelligence,
pleasant is avoiding of sins.

If we can strive to be our best self every day, then
we will be able to look back with joy on our lives
when we are older.

VERSE 37

He who, by causing pain to others, wishes to obtain pleasure for himself, he, entangled in the bonds of hatred, will never be free from hatred.

Any joy that we get at the expense of someone else's pain is tainted, and it will taint us in turn.

VERSE 38

Even in heavenly pleasures he finds no satisfaction, the disciple who is fully awakened delights only in the destruction of all desires.

Happiness comes from living a good life for its own sake rather than because we expect a reward in this life or the next.

58

VERSE 39

Health is the greatest of
gifts, contentedness the best
riches; trust is the best of
relationships, Nirvana the
highest happiness.

Good health, friends we can trust, and gratitude for our
blessings may seem like simple concepts, but they are the
foundation for lasting happiness.

VERSE 40

Wise people, after they have listened to the laws, become serene, like a deep, smooth, and still lake.

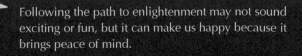

Following the path to enlightenment may not sound exciting or fun, but it can make us happy because it brings peace of mind.

VERSE 41

If a man is tossed about by doubts, full of strong passions, and yearning only for what is delightful, his thirst will grow more and more, and he will indeed make his fetters strong.

Indulging negative emotions and worldly desires will not satisfy us. Instead, we will only wish for more and more and become their prisoners.

VERSE 42

Why do what you will regret? Why bring tears upon yourself? Do only what you do not regret, and fill yourself with joy.

Even though in the moment it can feel easier to give in, it's always better to stick to our principles and avoid doing what we know we will regret.

VERSE 43

If a man does what is good, let him do it again; let him delight in it: happiness is the outcome of good.

We are always happy when we know we are doing something good. To keep being happy, keep doing good work.

VERSE 44

For a while the fool's mischief tastes sweet, sweet as honey. But in the end it turns bitter. And how bitterly he suffers!

Doing something bad can feel good in the moment, but sooner or later it always comes back to harm us.

VERSE 45

There is no fire like passion, there is no shark
like hatred, there is no snare like folly, there
is no torrent like greed.

Negative emotions are particularly harmful
because they can feel so strong, overwhelming
us with their poison.

VERSE 46

Cherish the road of peace.

Peace is precious, and must be kept safe in our hearts, minds, and actions so that it may bring happiness into the world.

VERSE 47

He whose evil deeds are covered by good deeds, brightens up this world, like the moon when freed from clouds.

We can't avoid making mistakes, but we can strive to outnumber our bad deeds with good ones.

VERSE 48

The virtuous man delights in this world, and he delights in the next; he delights in both. He delights and rejoices, when he sees the purity of his own work.

Virtuousness comes from deriving real happiness from doing good works.

VIRTUE

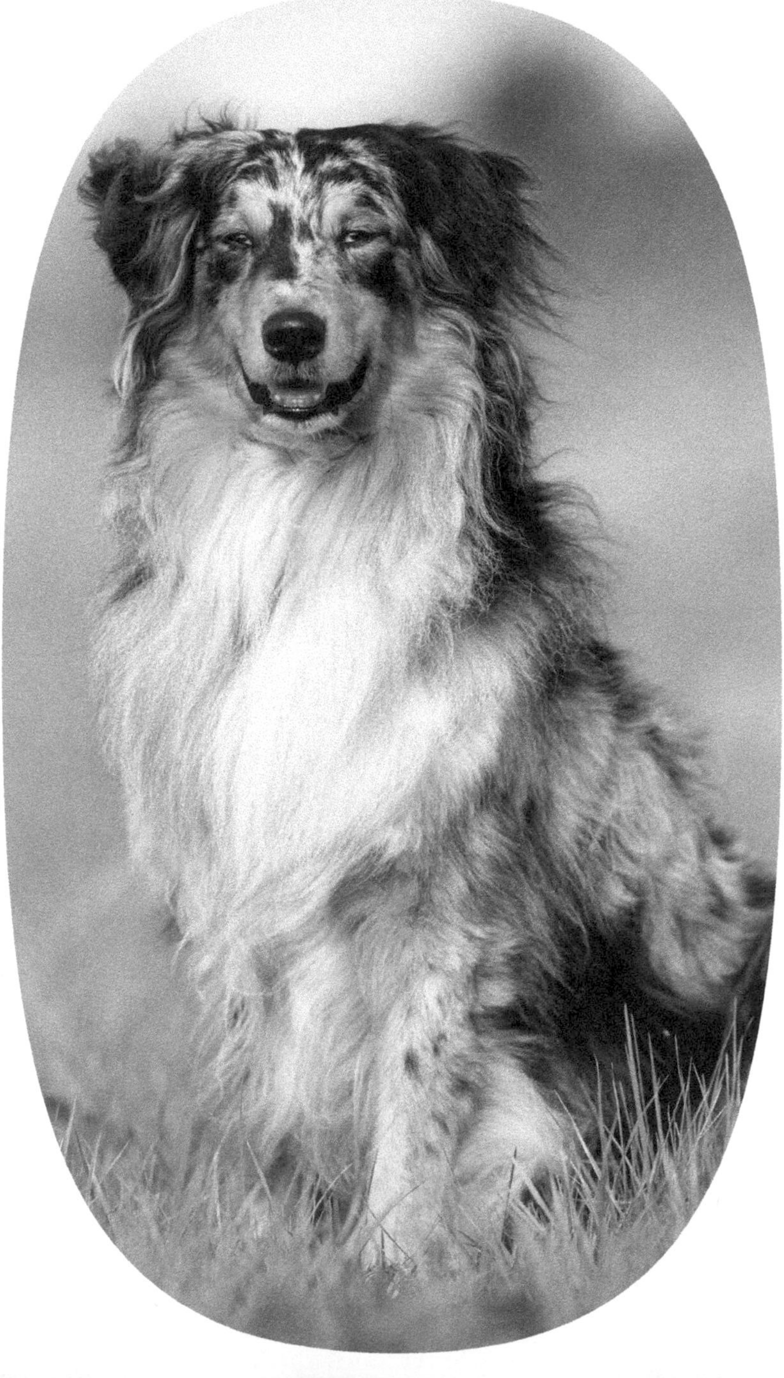

VERSE 49

The kind of seed sown will produce that kind of fruit. Those who do good will reap good results. Those who do evil will reap evil results. If you carefully plant a good seed, you will joyfully gather good fruit.

We get what we give to the world: to get joy and kindness, one must spread joy and kindness first.

VERSE 50

Even though a speech be a thousand words, but made up of senseless words, one word of sense is better, which if a man hears, he becomes quiet.

We must be careful with our words. Better to say nothing at all rather than to say something careless or destructive.

VERSE 51

The perfume of virtue travels against the wind and reaches into the ends of the world.

Virtue speaks for itself. If you do good works, the world can't help but notice.

VERSE 52

Let no one forget his own duty
for the sake of another's,
however great; let a man,
after he has discovered his
own duty, be always attentive
to his duty.

You can't control other people's actions, so it is
better to focus on controlling your own.

VERSE 53

Not the perversities of others, not their sins of commission or omission, but his own misdeeds and negligences should a sage take notice of.

It's easy to point out when other people are wrong, but more important to focus on what we might be doing wrong.

VERSE 54

And he who lives a hundred years, ignorant and unrestrained, a life of one day is better if a man is wise and reflecting.

A life isn't valuable because it is long. We must focus on making each day count.

VERSE 55

He who has no wound on his hand, may touch
poison with his hand; poison does not affect
one who has no wound; nor is there evil for
one who does not commit evil.

Evil only has the power we allow. Focus on forgiveness
and inner peace and evil cannot enter your heart.

VERSE 56

Look not for recognition, but follow the awakened. And set yourself free.

Concern for what others think can constrain you. Have confidence in your principles and follow your heart.

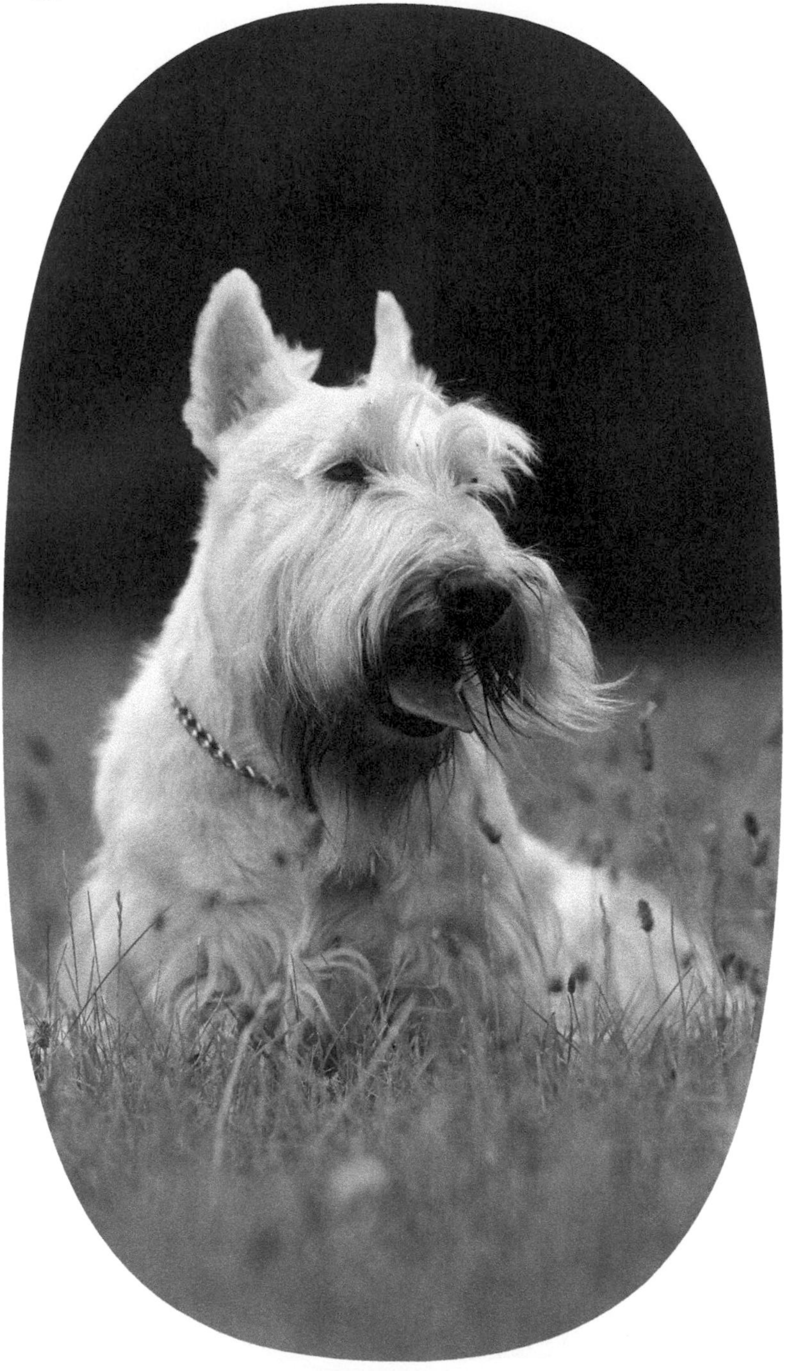

VERSE 57

Be quick to do good. If you are slow, the mind, delighting in mischief, will catch you.

Neglecting or procrastinating our responsibilities leads us down a bad path.

VERSE 58

Do not speak harshly to anybody; Angry speech is painful, blows for blows will touch thee.

Speaking in anger is a kind of violence, and can lead to everyone getting hurt.

VERSE 59

The evil done by oneself, self-begotten, self-bred, crushes the foolish, as a diamond breaks a precious stone.

When we do bad deeds, we hurt ourselves as much as we hurt others.

VERSE 60

Is there in this world any man so restrained by humility that he does not mind reproof, as a well-trained horse the whip?

It is important to learn how to take criticism, and not be so sensitive that we cannot learn from it.

VERSE 61

The disciple will find out the plainly shown path of virtue, as a clever man finds out the right flower.

Practicing virtuous behavior gives us good instincts to know right from wrong in future.

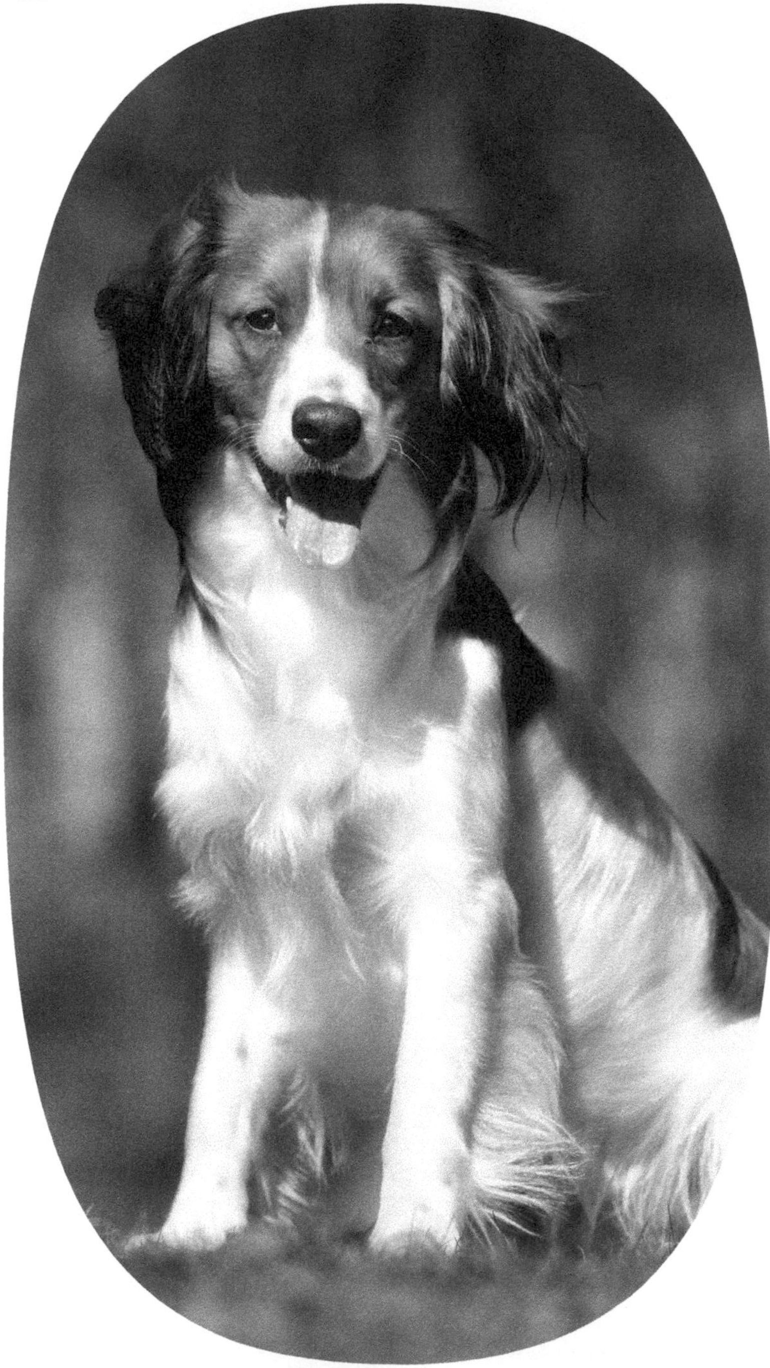

VERSE 62

Good people walk on whatever
befall, the good do not
prattle, longing for pleasure.

Instead of wasting time wishing things were better,
focus on the present and how you can improve it.

VERSE 63

Let no man think lightly of good, saying in his heart, It will not come nigh unto me. Even by the falling of water-drops a water-pot is filled; the wise man becomes full of good, even if he gather it little by little.

We become good people not by being perfect, but through little gestures of kindness accumulated every day.

VERSE 64

Let a man overcome anger by love, let him overcome evil by good; let him overcome the greedy by liberality, the liar by truth!

We cannot change the bad in the world, but we can counteract it by spreading goodness instead.

VERSE 65

An act carelessly performed, a broken vow,
and hesitating obedience to discipline, all
this brings no great reward.

It can be tempting to behave badly for short-term
gain, but we will be happier in the long run if we
do the right thing.

VERSE 66

By oneself the evil is done, by oneself one suffers; by oneself evil is left undone, by oneself one is purified. Purity and impurity belong to oneself, no one can purify another.

We cannot fix other people's hearts any more than they can fix ours. We must focus on being our own role models.

VERSE 67

Fools follow after vanity, men of evil wisdom. The wise man keeps earnestness as his best jewel.

Watch out for bad councilors. Look for people who are sincere.

VERSE 68

As many kinds of wreaths can be made from a heap of flowers, so many good things may be accomplished by a mortal once he is born.

Our lives are an accumulation of our actions, so we had best work to make them good ones.

VERSE 69

Do not have evil-doers for friends, do not have low people for friends: have virtuous people for friends, have for friends the best of men.

Our friends have the power to influence us, so it is important to make sure they will lead us to good instead of evil.

VERSE 70

If a man offend a harmless, pure, and innocent person, the evil falls back upon that fool, like light dust thrown up against the wind.

If someone tries to do you harm, do not rise to the bait. Your graciousness will make them look foolish.

VERSE 71

Well-makers lead the water; fletchers bend the arrow; carpenters bend a log of wood; good people fashion themselves.

Good people are made, not born. There is always time to work on becoming a good person.

VERSE 72

Good people shine from afar,
like the snowy mountains; bad
people are not seen, like arrows
shot by night.

Goodness projects a bright aura that draws people in,
spreading positive influence while evil is quickly forgotten.

TRUTH

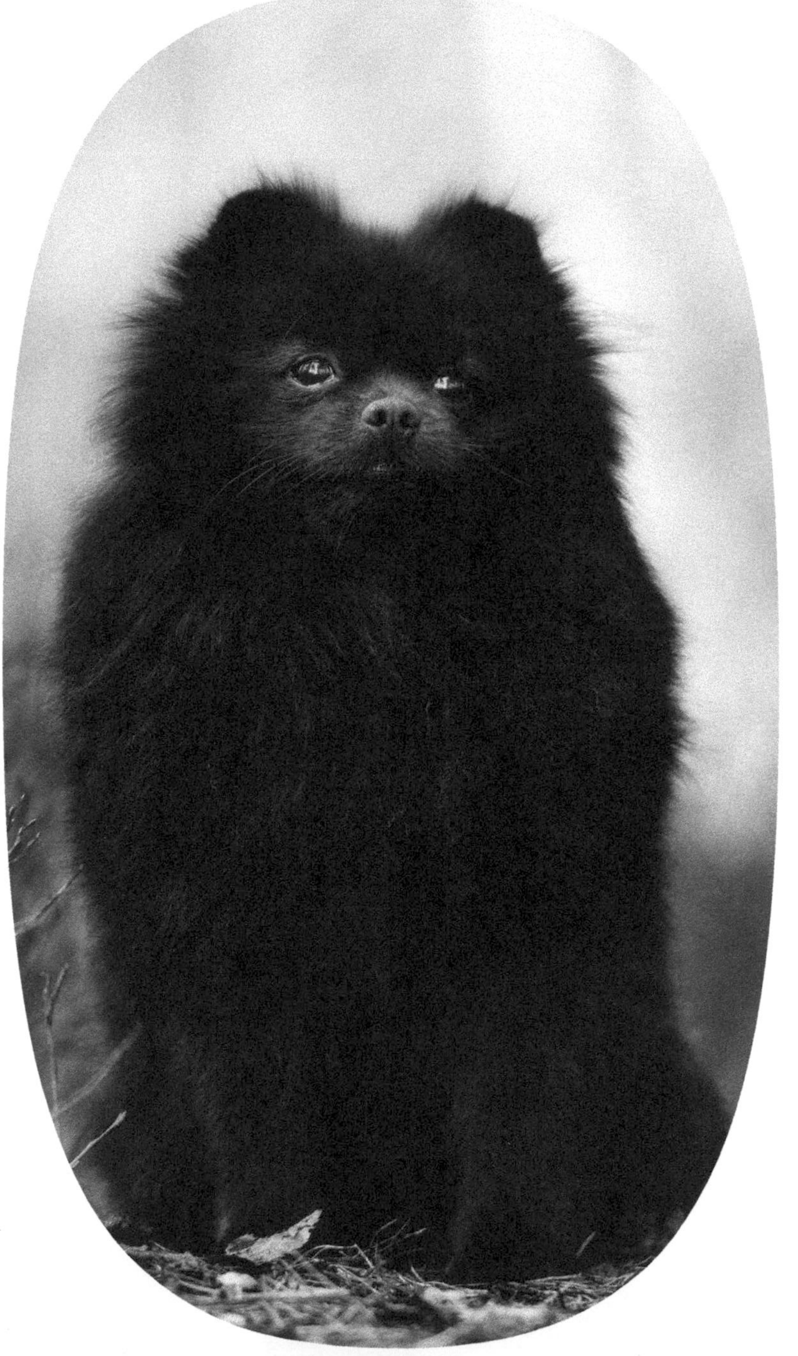

VERSE 73

Do not look for bad company
or live with men who do not
care. Find friends who love
the truth.

Choose friends who are engaged with learning the truth
instead of indifferent to it.

VERSE 74

The fields are damaged by weeds, mankind is damaged by vanity: therefore a gift bestowed on those who are free from vanity brings great reward.

Vanity warps our perception. When we free ourselves from it, we are better able to appreciate ourselves and others.

VERSE 75

For hatred does not cease by hatred at any time: hatred ceases by love, this is an old rule.

Choosing love and forgiveness is the only way to break the painful cycle of hatred.

VERSE 76

They who imagine truth in untruth, and see untruth in truth, never arrive at truth, but follow vain desires.

It is easy to twist facts to make them suit our worldview. Be open to seeing the world as it really is.

VERSE 77

The master finds freedom from desire
and sorrow - Freedom without bounds.

When we stop allowing our negative emotions to
hold us back, we are able to see the world in new,
exciting ways.

VERSE 78

So was my past existence at that time real,
but unreal the future and present existence;
and my future existence will be at one
time real, but unreal the past and present
existence; and my present existence is now
real, but unreal the past and future existence.

Whoever we have been in the past and whoever we
may be in the future is beyond our control. We can only
decide who we want to be right now.

VERSE 79

The fool who knows his foolishness, is
wise at least so far. But a fool who thinks
himself wise, he is called a fool indeed.

Be aware that your knowledge has limits, and that
there is always more to learn.

VERSE 80

Let each man direct himself first to what
is proper, then let him teach others;
thus a wise man will not suffer.

Before telling others what to do, make sure that you
have made yourself the best you can be.

VERSE 81

As a solid rock is not shaken by the wind, wise
people falter not amidst blame and praise.

We should do the right thing for its own sake without
seeking admiration or being afraid of criticism.

VERSE 82

Do not follow the evil law! Do not live on in
thoughtlessness! Do not follow false doctrine!
Be not a friend of the world.

Do not blindly follow what you are told. Consult
your sense of right and wrong.

VERSE 83

Speak the truth, do not
yield to anger; give if thou
art asked for little; by these
three steps thou wilt go near
the gods.

If we are generous, free of resentment, and remain sincere,
then we will be living a spiritual life.

VERSE 84

A man is not learned because he talks much; he who is patient, free from hatred and fear, he is called learned.

Being intelligent doesn't mean showing off. It means knowing how to control ourselves so that we do the right thing at the right time.

VERSE 85

They who fear when they ought not to fear, and fear not when they ought to fear, such men, embracing false doctrines, enter the evil path.

A little fear is healthy, but too much will hold us back. We must learn to control our fear so that it doesn't lead us astray.

VERSE 86

Without knowledge, there is no meditation, without meditation there is no knowledge: he who has knowledge and meditation is near unto Nirvana.

Take time to consider what you learn. Through contemplation, we find understanding and enlightenment.

VERSE 87

Him I call enlightened who utters true speech, instructive and free from harshness, so that he offend no one.

When we are teaching others, it is important to do so with kindness and humility so that our message is not lost in pride or resentment.

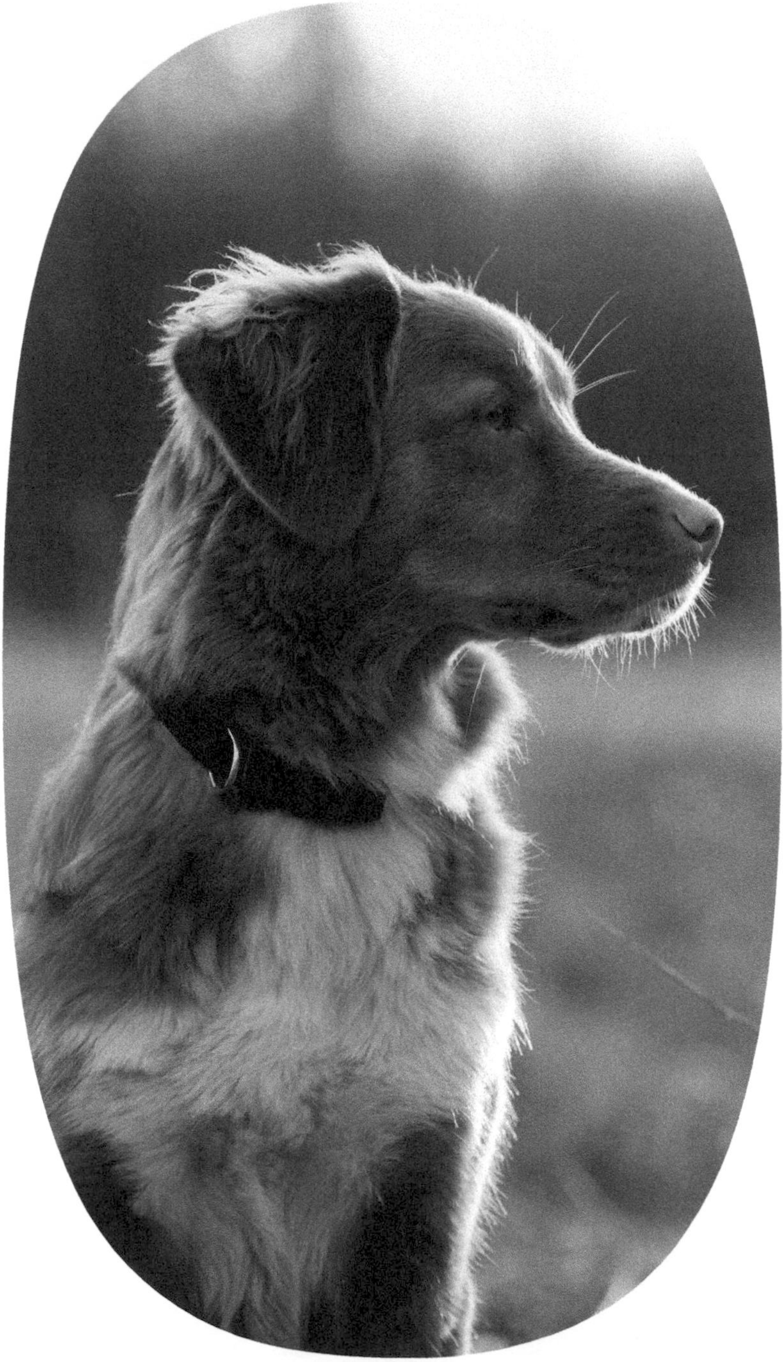

VERSE 88

He abused me, he beat me, he defeated me, he robbed me,'—in those who harbor such thoughts hatred will never cease.

Holding on to past grievances poisons us with negative emotions. The only way to free ourselves is to forgive.

VERSE 89

Few are there among men who arrive at the other shore; the other people here run up and down the shore.

It is not enough to identify the right path. We must find the courage to take it.

VERSE 90

Bad deeds, and deeds hurtful to ourselves, are easy to do; what is beneficial and good, that is very difficult to do.

We must follow our consciences away from bad paths even when they tempt us.

VERSE 91

Your worst enemy cannot harm you as much as your own thoughts, unguarded. But once mastered, no one can help you as much, not even your father or your mother.

Our minds can turn against us, replaying bad memories, thoughts, and emotions. But if we control them, they give us the power to find good in anything.

VERSE 92

In overcoming wrong action with attentive mind, and dwelling with attentive mind in possession of right action, one practices Right Attentiveness.

We must examine our actions to be sure that they are coming from good motives instead of bad ones.

VERSE 93

Men, driven by fear, go to many a refuge, to mountains and forests, to groves and sacred trees. But that is not a safe refuge, that is not the best refuge; a man is not delivered from all pains after having gone to that refuge.

Running away from problems means you will live in fear of them forever. Facing them gives you the chance to conquer your fear.

VERSE 94

Develop your concentration: for he who
has concentration understands things
according to their reality.

Being completely focused on our lives and in our
meditations helps us understand them better.

VERSE 95

By watching and working, the master makes for himself an island, which the flood cannot overwhelm.

Life can seem overwhelming, but by fortifying our minds and spirits we build a protection that can't be broken.

VERSE 96

How can a troubled mind understand the way? If a man is disturbed, he will never be filled with knowledge.

We must learn to let go of our fears, concerns, and distractions. They impede our ability to learn from the present and move forward.

ETERNITY

VERSE 97

Better than a hundred years of mischief is one day spent in contemplation.

Time spent thinking is never wasted. Consider before acting in haste.

VERSE 98

Yielding like the earth, Joyous and clear
like the lake, Still as the stone at the
door, He is free from life and death.

By maintaining a peaceful balance in our hearts and
minds, we will have nothing to fear from life or death.

VERSE 99

When your light shines without impurity
or desire, you will come into the
boundless country.

When your spirit is cleansed of negative
emotions and experiences, then you will
arrive in a spiritual state.

VERSE 100

There is no suffering for him who has finished his journey, and abandoned grief, who has freed himself on all sides, and thrown off all fetters.

Rather than fearing death, rejoice in the knowledge that human pain and suffering does not follow.

VERSE 101

Give up the old ways -
Passion, enmity, folly. Know
the truth and find peace.

When we refuse to harbor negative emotions, then we
achieve lasting inner peace.

VERSE 102

Let him live in charity, let him be perfect in his duties; then in the fullness of delight he will make an end of suffering.

Our suffering ends when we find peace, and the best way to find peace is to conduct ourselves with honor.

VERSE 103

When one understands that corporeality,
feeling, perception, mental formation,
and consciousness, are transient, also
in that case one possesses Right
Understanding.

All things pass away in time, so do not dwell on the
evil and appreciate the good.

VERSE 104

The extinction of greed, the extinction of anger, the extinction of delusion: this, indeed, is called Nirvana.

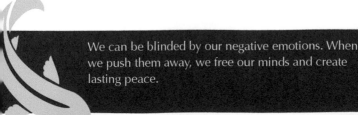

We can be blinded by our negative emotions. When we push them away, we free our minds and create lasting peace.

VERSE 105

This world is dark, few only can see here; a few only go on to heaven, like birds escaped from the net.

Transcending our earthly limitations is difficult, but spiritual enlightenment brings true freedom.

VERSE 106

Give up what is before, give up
what is behind, give up what is
in the middle, when thou goest
to the other shore of existence;
if thy mind is altogether free,
thou wilt not enter again into
birth and decay.

Learn to give up regret for the past, concern for the present, and
fear of the future. Acceptance is the way to lasting peace.

VERSE 107

Here I shall dwell in the rain, here in winter and summer,' thus the fool meditates, and does not think of his death.

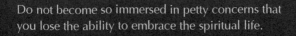

Do not become so immersed in petty concerns that you lose the ability to embrace the spiritual life.

VERSE 108

Men who have not observed proper discipline, and have not gained treasure in their youth, perish like old herons in a lake without fish.

Being a good person is the work of a lifetime. Do not wait until you are older to begin.

VERSE 109

All men tremble at punishment, all men love
life; remember that thou art like unto them,
and do not kill nor cause slaughter.

Every life is precious, so refrain from taking one.

VERSE 110

You too shall pass away. Knowing this,
how can you quarrel? How easily the wind
overturns a frail tree.

When we remember that life is short, we realize that
fighting is a waste of time.

VERSE 111

The evil-doer mourns in this world, and he mourns in the next; he mourns in both. He mourns and suffers when he sees the evil of his own work.

Evil leaves a lasting impression on the person who commits the crime.

VERSE 112

All created things perish. He who knows and
sees this becomes passive in pain; this is
the way to purity.

By accepting that everything ends, even pain, we
are harmed less by current suffering.

VERSE 113

Earnestness is the path to immortality,
thoughtlessness the path of death. Those
who are in earnest do not die, those who
are thoughtless are as if dead already.

When we are sincerely thoughtful to others, we are
cherished even after we die.

VERSE 114

He who knows that this body is like froth, and has learnt that it is as unsubstantial as a mirage, will break the flower-pointed arrow of Mara, and never see the king of death.

Do not be vain. A beautiful body is temporary, but a beautiful spirit is eternal.

VERSE 115

The brilliant chariots of kings are destroyed, the body also approaches destruction, but the virtue of good people never approaches destruction.

Money is temporary wealth. You cannot take it with you into the next world. Spiritual wealth is always with you.

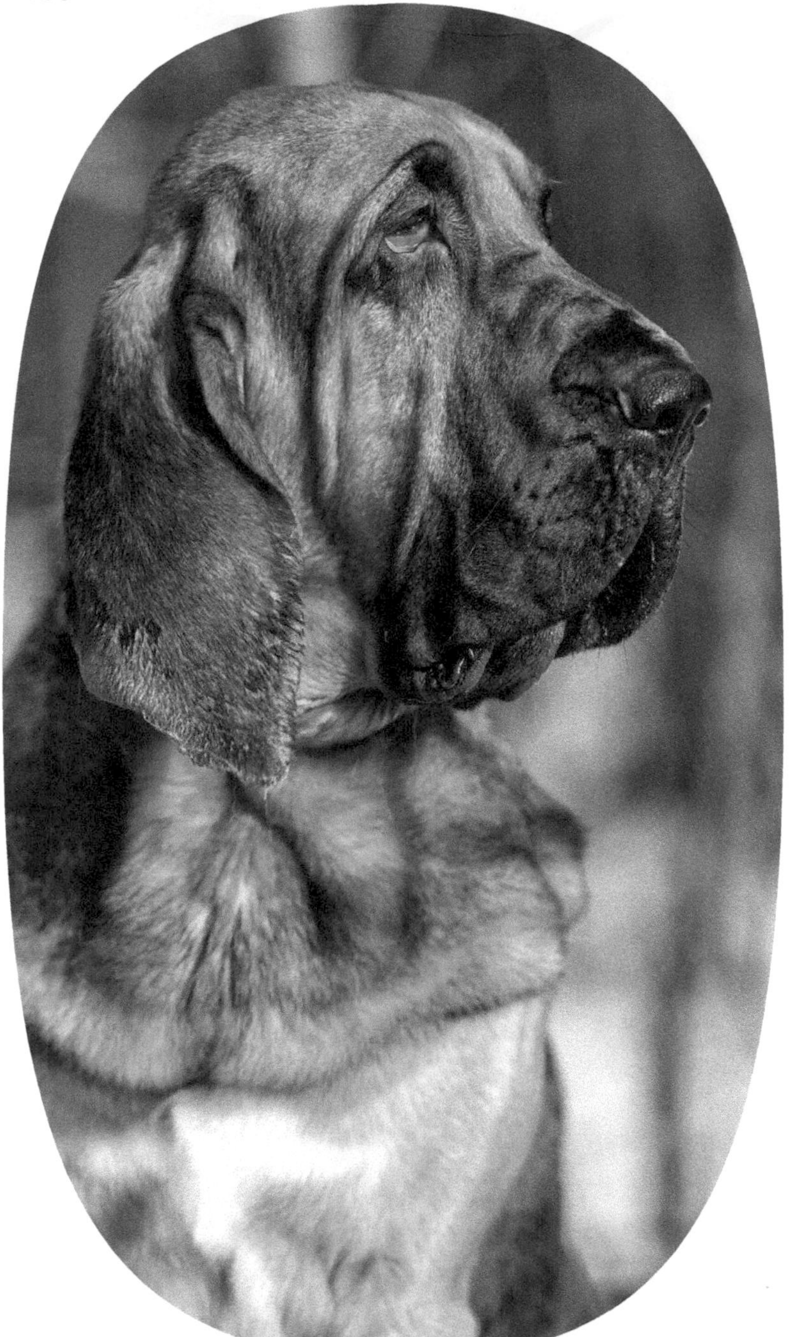

VERSE 116

For great is the harvest in this world, and greater still in the next.

Performing good works benefits us in this life, but our true reward comes in the afterlife.

VERSE 117

When you have understood the destruction of all that was made, you will understand that which was not made.

Once we accept that the material will fall apart, we realize what is spiritual, permanent, and valuable.

VERSE 118

Wakefulness is the way to life. The fool sleeps as if he were already dead, but the master is awake and he lives forever.

They who are alert to the spiritual path need not fear death, as their spirits will out live their bodies.

VERSE 119

Rouse thyself! Do not be idle! Follow the law of virtue! The virtuous rests in bliss in this world and in the next.

We must strive to be virtuous and do good works knowing that our time for rest will come in the next life.

VERSE 120

And he who lives a hundred years, not seeing the immortal place, a life of one day is better if a man sees the immortal place.

The life spent in pursuit of spirituality, no matter how long, is the most worthy.

CREDITS

All Photos from Shutterstock

* Not from Shutterstock